The Essential Keto Diet Cookbook for Beginners

2021

Table of Contents

4

INTRODUCTION

What you will find in this book

This book will give you complete information about the followings-

What is ketogenic diet?

Health Benefits of ketogenic diet.

Keto Misconceptions

How to reach Ketosis.

How to know if you have achieved ketosis.

Exercise on Ketogenic diet.

Ketogenic diet Macros.

Keto Lifestyle

Food Choice

Keto Recipes.

Why i wrote this book

I wrote this book so that I can share the knowledge of Ketogenic diet with everyone who wants to lose weight and live a healthy lifestyle. This book will help you to understand what is ketogenic diet and how your body acts in keto state. There are so many myths and doubts related to Ketogenic diet, all doubts will be resolved in this book.

My story with keto diet

By eating fewer carbs, you induce your body to the state of ketosis thus making it easier for the body to tap into the stored fat reserves it already has on hand. But getting yourself into the state of ketosis is never easy. Either you go on fasting for days or you cut down your carb intake to 50 grams daily, which is equivalent to around 5% of your total calories.

This can be achieved by changing your diet. Instead of taking in your usual diet, you can drive ketosis by eating more fat and protein. Your fat should be 60-75% of your daily calories while your protein intake should be 15-30% of your calories. This is equivalent to 1 large chicken breast and 5 small avocados each meal. Because fat is naturally filling, it will keep you full for a long time, so you will not feel the need to snack between meals.

The goal for the ketogenic diet is to get your body into the state of ketosis by breaking down fats into ketones as the primary source of fuel by eating the right amounts of food that support such metabolic pathway.

What weight loss is all about

The keto diet changes the way your body transforms food into energy. Eating lots of fat and low carbohydrates will put you in a metabolic state where your body burns fat instead of carbohydrates. If your body can not get glucose from carbs, your liver converts the fatty acids in your diet into ketones, an alternative energy source. The burning of ketones instead of glucose leads to reduced inflammation and stimulates weight loss.

Chapter 4: Breakfast Recipes

Keto Pancakes

Preparation time: 25 minutes

Servings: 5

Ingredients:

5 eggs

½ tsp baking powder

2 scoops stevia

¼ cup coconut flour

¼ cup water

4 tbsp coconut oil, solid

1 tbsp vanilla extract

Keto cooking spray

Directions:

Take an electric griddle and heat it to 375 degrees F.

Crack eggs in a bowl and stir in all the remaining Ingredients.

Whisk well to combine and pour ¼th of the pancake batter into the pan.

Cook the pancake for about 3 minutes on one side.

Flip over and cook the other side for about 3 minutes.

Repeat with the remaining mixture and serve.

Nutritional Values

Calories 189 kcal

Total Fat 15.9 g

Saturated Fat 11.2 g

Cholesterol 164 mg

Sodium 63 mg

Total Carbs 4.9 g

Fiber 2.4 g

Sugar 0.7 g

Protein 6.3 g

Avocado and Salmon

Preparation time: 15 minutes

Serves: 3

Meal Type: Appetizer

Ingredients:

2 medium-sized Avocados

¼ cup of Keto Mayo

¼ cup of grated of grated Parmesan cheese

1/3 teaspoons of Paprika

1/3 teaspoons of pepper

½ cup of cheddar cheese

1 tablespoon of Chives

4 ounces of salmon fillets

1 spoon of olive oil

Directions:

Cut the avocado in two and take out the pit. Set aside

Preheat the oven to 350°

Mix the Keto mayo and salmon.

Add the oil and stir well

Put the mix in the avocados

Sprinkle with pepper

Bake at to 300° for 5 minutes

Put the cheese in a microwave safe bowl.

Put in till melted

Smear generously on the avocados

Toss chives and Paprika on them

Bacon and Eggs

Preparation time: 10 minutes

Serves: 1

Meal Type: Breakfast

Ingredients:

3 eggs

Salt and pepper

3 spoons of shredded cheese

5 ounces of sliced bacon

3 spoons of olive oil

3 spoons of ghee

Cherry tomatoes

Fresh parsley

Directions:

Crack and mix eggs

Season with salt and pepper

Heat fry pan

Put in ghee and oil in a pan

Put in bacon and fry

When fried, use the same pot to fry the eggs

Turn off the heat and toss in the cheese to melt

Put your bacon in and stir

Serve warm

Cauliflowers

Preparation time: 2hrs

Serves 4

Ingredients

4 oz. Cheddar cheese

1/8 teaspoon salt

3 eggs

1/2 leek, cut into quarter inch half-moon slices

6 cooked sausage links, cut into quarter inch rounds

2.5 oz. cremini mushrooms, finely diced

1/8 teaspoon salt

5 oz. cauliflower florets

Directions

Grease a crockpot with cooking spray and set aside. Meanwhile add pieces of the cauliflower to a heat-safe bowl along with salt.

Add water to the bowl and fill it to entirely cover the cauliflower, and put it in the microwave to cook for about 8 minutes.

As it cooks, be preparing the leeks, sausage and mushrooms. Then drain off the liquid from the half cooked cauliflower and add it to the crockpot.

Evenly distribute the sausage and mushrooms pieces on the cauliflower and set aside.

Now whisk together salt and eggs in a bowl and carefully stir in cleaned leeks. Slowly stir in half of the cheese and reserve the other half.

Then pour the egg mixture uniformly over the cauliflower pieces, sausage and the mushrooms.

Cover the Ingredients and cook on high for about 2 to 3 hours, or until the eggs puff up.

At this point, sprinkle the rest of the cheese over the top and allow it to melt. Then slice the casserole and enjoy. Season the dish with salt and pepper if you like.

Nutritional Information per Serving: Calories 356.5, Fat 29.9g, Carbs 4.5g, Protein 18.9g

Frittata with Spinach

Preparation time: 1 hr

Serves 3

Ingredients

1/2 Roma tomato, diced

Salt to taste

1/2 cup chopped baby spinach, without stems

1/8 teaspoon white pepper

1/8 teaspoon black pepper

1 tablespoon coconut milk

2 egg whites

2 eggs

1/2 cup 2% shredded mozzarella cheese, divided

1/4 cup diced onion

1/2 tablespoon extra-virgin olive oil

Directions

Add oil to a small skillet and sauté the onion for around 5 minutes. Once tender, remove from the skillet and set aside.

With non-stick cooking spray, coat a slow cooker and set aside.

Mix together ¾ of the cheese, sautéed onion and the rest of the **Ingredients**. Whisk to combine and transfer to the Crockpot.

Now sprinkle with the remaining mozzarella on top of the mixture. Cook the contents on low for 1 hour to 1 ½ hours while covered.

As soon as the eggs are set, remove from the cooker and serve.

Nutritional Information per Serving: Carbs: 4g, Calories: 139, Fat: 8g, Protein: 12g

Creamy Eggs

Preparation Time: 5 minutes

Serve: 1

Ingredients:

2 eggs

1 tbsp heavy whipping cream

1 tbsp chives, chopped

1 oz cheddar cheese, shredded

1 oz butter

1/4 tsp pepper

1/2 tsp salt

Directions:

Melt butter in a pan over medium heat.

Whisk eggs together with heavy whipping cream, pepper, and salt.

Pour the egg mixture into the pan and stir for 3-4 minutes.

Add cheddar cheese and stir until cheese is melted.

Garnish with chopped chives and serve.

Nutritional Value (Amount per Serving):

Calories 495

Fat 45 g

Carbohydrates 2 g

Sugar 1 g

Protein 17 g

Cholesterol 439 mg

Beef Meatloaf

Preparation Time: 10 minutes

Serve: 8

Ingredients:

2 eggs

2 lbs ground beef

½ cup marinara sauce, sugar-free and homemade

3/4 cup cottage cheese

1 lb mozzarella cheese, cut into hunks

2 tsp Italian seasoning

¼ cup basil pesto

½ cup parmesan cheese, grated

¼ tsp pepper

1 tsp salt

Directions:

Preheat the oven to 400 F.

Add all **Ingredients** into the large bowl and mix until well combined.

Transfer bowl mixture to the greased casserole dish and bake for 40 minutes.

Serve and enjoy.

Nutritional Value (Amount per Serving):

Calories 351

Fat 19 g

Carbohydrates 4 g

Sugar 2 g

Zucchini Spread

Preparation time: 10 minutes

Servings: 4

Ingredients:

4 zucchinis, sliced

A pinch of salt and black pepper

½ cup heavy cream

½ cup cream cheese, soft

2 garlic cloves, minced

½ cup veggie stock

1 tablespoon avocado oil

1 tablespoon dill, chopped

Directions:

In your instant pot, mix the zucchinis with the stock, salt and pepper, put the lid on and cook on High for 12 minutes.

Release the pressure naturally for 10 minutes, drain the zucchinis, transfer them to a blender, add the rest of the

Ingredients, pulse, divide into bowls and serve as a morning spread.

Cheese Muffins

Preparation time: 45 minutes

Serves: 6

Ingredients

1 ½ cups double cream

5 ounces goat cheese, crumbled

3 eggs, beaten

Salt and black pepper, to taste

1 tbsp butter, softened

2 cups mushrooms, chopped

2 garlic cloves, minced

Directions

Preheat the oven to 320°F. Insert 6 ramekins into a large pan. Add in boiling water up to 1-inch depth.In a pan, over medium heat, warm double cream. Set heat to a simmer; stir in goat cheese and cook until melted.

Set the beaten eggs in a bowl and place in 3 tablespoons of the hot cream mixture; combine well. Place the mixture back to the pan with hot cream/cheese mixture.

Sprinkle with pepper and salt. Ladle the mixture into ramekins. Bake for 40 minutes.

Spread the a, jillo mushrooms on top of each cooled muffin to serve.

Keto Waffles

Preparation Time: 10 minutes

Serve: 4

Ingredients:

8 drops liquid stevia

1/2 tsp baking soda

1 tbsp chia seeds

1/4 cup water

2 tbsp sunflower seed butter

1 tsp cinnamon

1 avocado, peel, pitted and mashed

1 tsp vanilla

1 tbsp lemon juice

3 tbsp coconut flour

Directions:

Preheat the waffle iron.

In a small bowl, add water and chia seeds and soak for 5 minutes.

Mash together sunflower seed butter, lemon juice, vanilla, stevia, chia mixture, and avocado.

Mix together cinnamon, baking soda, and coconut flour.

Add wet **Ingredients** to the dry **Ingredients** and mix well.

Pour waffle mixture into the hot waffle iron and cook on each side for 3-5 minutes.

Serve and enjoy.

Baked Granola

Preparation time: 30 minutes

Serves: 3

Ingredients:

1 cup of flaxseeds

Directions*:*

Beat the egg

Preheat oven to 300 degrees F

Set out a bowl and put in all Ingredients

Set out a baking pan with parchment paper

Pour **Ingredients** in

Bake for 30 minutes

Chapter 5: Keto Recipes for Lunch

Beef Salad

Preparation Time: 15 minutes

Servings 4

Ingredients

1/2 pound beef rump steak, cut into strips

1/2 teaspoon sea salt

1/3 teaspoon freshly cracked black pepper

1 teaspoon soy sauce

2 tablespoons sesame oil

1 red onion, peeled and sliced

1 garlic clove, minced

1 bunch fresh mint

2 avocados, pitted, peeled and sliced

2 cucumbers, sliced

1 bunch fresh Thai basil, leaves picked

1 teaspoon minced Thai chili

2 tablespoons rice vinegar

1 tablespoon fresh lime juice

1/4 cup pumpkin seeds

Directions

Combine the beef with the salt, pepper and soy sauce.

Preheat the oil in a nonstick skillet over medium-low heat. Then, sauté the onion and garlic until tender and aromatic, about 4 minutes.

Cook the beef on a grill pan for 5 minutes or until cooked to your liking.

Arrange the fresh mint, avocado slices, cucumber, Thai basil, and Thai chili in a nice salad bowl. Top with the beef slices. Add the onion-garlic mixture.

Drizzle with rice vinegar and lime juice. Sprinkle with pumpkin seeds and serve.

Turkey Salad

Preparation time: 20 minutes

Servings: 6

Ingredients

1 pound ground turkey

1 tablespoon olive oil

Salt and ground black pepper, as required

¼ cup water

½ of English cucumber, chopped

4 cups green cabbage, shredded

½ cup fresh mint leaves, chopped

2 tablespoons fresh lime juice

¼ cup walnuts, chopped

Directions

Heat the oil in a skillet over medium-high heat and cook the turkey for about 6-8 minutes, breaking up the meat with a spatula.

Stir in the salt, black pepper, and water and cook for about 4-5 minutes or until almost all the liquid is evaporated.

Remove from heat and transfer the turkey into a bowl.

Set the bowl aside to cool completely.

In a large serving bowl, mix well vegetables, mint and lime juice.

Add the cooked turkey and stir to combine.

Top with the chopped walnuts and serve.

Beef Meatballs

Preparation time: 15 Minutes

Serving: 8

Ingredients:

1.5 lb of ground beef

Two tablespoon parsley (chopped)

One teaspoon oregano (dried)

Two spring onions (chopped)

½ cup parmesan cheese (sharply grated)

Two eggs

One teaspoon garlic (puree)

½ cup almond flour

Two tablespoon water

Salt, as you like

For Meatball Sauce:

Two tablespoon of red wine vinegar

2*14 ounces tomatoes (chopped)

One teaspoon of Herbs de Provence

Three tablespoon of water

One tablespoon of olive oil

Directions:

Combine all the **Ingredients** together in a meatball, except for **Ingredients** for the sauce. Mix it well.

Make the 1 inch round meatball using your hands.

Select the sauté setting and add oil and meatballs in it and brown them well. Work in batches, so the meatballs don't get ruined.

Pour the tomatoes, vinegar, herbs and water over the meatballs and close the lid.

Close the lid and cook the meatballs for five minutes on high-pressure mode.

When the cooking is done, let the steam release manually for ten minutes then quickly release the remaining pressure.

Your meatballs are ready to enjoy them with zoodles or cauliflower rice.

Nutritional Data Per Serving:

Fat: 25 gram

Fiber: 1 gram

Carbohydrates: 6 gram

Protein: 20 gram

Sugar: 2 gram

Shrimp and Zucchini

Preparation Time: 15 minutes

Servings: 4

Ingredients

2 tablespoons unsalted butter

1 large garlic clove, minced

¼ teaspoon red pepper flakes, crushed

1 pound medium shrimp, peeled and deveined

Salt and ground black pepper, as required

1/3 cup homemade chicken broth

2 medium zucchinis, spiralized with blade C

1 tablespoon fresh parsley, finely chopped

Directions:

Melt the butter in a large skillet over medium heat and sauté the garlic and red pepper flakes for about 1 minute.

Add the shrimp, salt, and black pepper and cook for about 1 minute per side.

Add the broth and zucchini noodles and cook for about 3-4 minutes, tossing occasionally.

Garnish with fresh parsley and serve hot.

Beef Curry

Preparation Time: 10 minutes

Serve: 4

Ingredients:

2 lbs stewing beef, cut into cubes

1/2 tsp coriander

1 tsp cumin

1 tbsp garam masala

1 tsp turmeric

1 tbsp olive oil

1/2 tsp lemon zest

1tsp paprika

1/2 tsp cayenne pepper

2 garlic cloves, minced

1 onion, chopped

1/4 cup fresh cilantro, chopped

1/2 cup tomatoes, crushed

1/2 cup beef stock

1 tsp pepper

1 tsp salt

Directions:

Heat oil in a pan over medium heat.

Add garlic and onion and sauté for 5 minutes.

Add spices, pepper, and salt and stir for minute.

Stir in crushed tomatoes and transfer pan mixture into the blender and blend until smooth.

Place meat into the crock pot and pour sauce mixture, stock, and lemon zest over meat.

Cover and cook on low for 6 hours.

Garnish with cilantro and serve.

Broccoli Soup

Preparation Time: 10 minutes

Serve: 4

Ingredients:

2/3 lb broccoli florets

3 1/4 vegetable stock

1/2 lb cream cheese

1 leek, chopped

2 garlic cloves, chopped

½ cup fresh basil

3 oz olive oil

Pepper

Salt

Directions:

Add broccoli, leek, salt, and stock in saucepan. Bring to boil.

Transfer broccoli mixture in blender with olive oil, cream cheese, pepper and basil and blend until smooth.

Serve and enjoy.

Pumpkin Soup

Preparation Time: 10 minutes

Serve: 4

Ingredients:

2 cups pumpkin, diced

1/2 tsp paprika

2 cups vegetable stock

1 tsp olive oil

2 garlic cloves, minced

1 tomato, chopped

1 onion, chopped

2 tsp curry powder

Salt

Directions:

In a saucepan, add oil, garlic, and onion and sauté for 3 minutes over medium heat.

Add remaining **Ingredients** and bring to boil.

Reduce heat and cover and simmer for 10 minutes.

Puree the soup using a blender until smooth.

Serve and enjoy.

Meatballs and Pilaf

Preparation Time: 40 minutes

Servings: 4

Ingredients:

1 pound lamb; ground

4 ounces goat cheese; crumbled

1 egg

12 ounces cauliflower florets

2 garlic cloves; minced

2 tablespoons coconut oil

1 bunch mint; chopped.

1 tablespoon lemon zest

1 teaspoon fennel seed

1 teaspoon paprika

1 teaspoon garlic powder

1 small yellow onion; chopped.

Salt and black pepper to the taste.

Directions:

Put cauliflower florets in your food processor, add salt and pulse well.

Grease a pan with some of the coconut oil, heat up over medium heat; add cauliflower rice, cook for 8 minutes, season with salt and pepper to the taste., take off heat and keep warm.

In a bowl, mix lamb with salt, pepper, egg, paprika, garlic powder and fennel seed and stir very well.

Shape 12 meatballs and place them on a plate for now.

Heat up a pan with the coconut oil over medium heat; add onion; stir and cook for 6 minutes

Add garlic; stir and cook for 1 minute

Add meatballs, cook them well on all sides and take off heat.

Divide cauliflower rice between plates, add meatballs and onion mix on top, sprinkle mint, lemon zest and goat cheese at the end and serve

Caprese Salad

Preparation Time: 5 minutes

Servings: 2

Ingredients:

1/2 pound mozzarella cheese, sliced

1 tablespoon balsamic vinegar

1 tablespoon olive oil

1 tomato, sliced

4 basil leaves, torn

Salt and black pepper to the taste.

Directions:

Alternate tomato and mozzarella slices on 2 plates

Sprinkle salt, pepper, drizzle vinegar and olive oil.

Sprinkle basil leaves at the end and serve

Chapter 6: Keto Recipes for Dinner

Caesar Salad

Preparation time: 10 minutes

Serving: 16

Ingredients

1 organic egg yolk

2 tablespoons fresh lemon juice

1 tablespoon anchovy paste

2 teaspoons Dijon mustard

2 garlic cloves, peeled

1 tablespoon fresh oregano

Salt and ground black pepper, as required

½ cup olive oil

½ cup Parmesan cheese, shredded

Directions

Place all the Ingredients except oil and Parmesan in a blender and pulse until smooth.

While the motor is running gradually, add the oil and pulse until smooth.

Add the Parmesan cheese and pulse for about 20 seconds.

Serve immediately.

Chicken Bowls

Preparation time: 10 minutes

Servings: 4

Ingredients:

1 avocado, peeled and cut into wedges

2 tomatoes, cubed

1 and ½ cups baby spinach

A pinch of salt and black pepper

2 chicken breasts, skinless, boneless and cubed

2 tablespoons olive oil

2 tablespoons chicken stock

¼ cup tomato passata

1 shallot, chopped

Directions:

Set your instant pot on sauté mode, add the oil, heat it up, add the shallot and sauté for 2 minutes.

Add the chicken, stock and tomato passata, put the lid on and cook on High for 13 minutes.

Release the pressure naturally for 10 minutes, transfer the chicken mix to a bowl, add the remaining **Ingredients**, toss and serve for breakfast.

Feta Kale Frittata

Preparation Time: 10 minutes

Serve: 8

Ingredients:

8 eggs, beaten

4 oz feta cheese, crumbled

6 oz bell pepper, roasted and diced

5 oz baby kale

1/4 cup green onion, sliced

2 tsp olive oil

Directions:

Heat olive oil in a pan over medium-high heat.

Add kale to the pan and sauté for 4-5 minutes or until softened.

Spray slow cooker with cooking spray.

Add cooked kale into the slow cooker.

Add green onion and bell pepper into the slow cooker.

Pour beaten eggs into the slow cooker and stir well to combine.

Sprinkle crumbled feta cheese.

Cook on low for 2 hours or until frittata is set.

Serve and enjoy.

Broccoli Nuggets

Preparation Time: 10 minutes

Serve: 4

Ingredients:

2 egg whites

2 cups broccoli florets

1/4 cup almond flour

1 cup cheddar cheese, shredded

1/8 tsp salt

Directions:

Preheat the oven to 350 F.

Add broccoli in bowl and mash using masher.

Add remaining **Ingredients** to the broccoli and mix well.

Drop 20 scoops onto baking tray and press lightly down.

Bake in preheated oven for 20 minutes.

Serve and enjoy

Coconut Porridge

Preparation Time: 7 minutes

Servings: 4

Ingredients:

1 cup coconut milk

3 tablespoons blackberries

2 tablespoons walnuts

1 teaspoon butter

1 teaspoon ground cinnamon

5 tablespoons chia seeds

3 tablespoons coconut flakes

¼ teaspoon salt

Directions:

Pour the coconut milk into the air fryer basket tray. Add the coconut, salt, chia seeds, ground cinnamon, and butter. Ground up the walnuts and add them to the air fryer basket tray. Sprinkle the mixture with salt. Mash the blackberries with a fork and add them also to the air fryer basket tray. Cook the porridge at 375°Fahrenheit for 7-minutes. When the cook time is over, remove the air fryer basket from air fryer and allow to sit and rest for 5-minutes. Stir porridge with a wooden spoon and serve warm.

Nutritional Values per serving: Calories: 169, Total Fat: 18.2g, Carbs: 9.3g, Protein: 4.2g

Cheese Broccoli Bread

Preparation Time: 10 minutes

Serve: 5

Ingredients:

5 eggs, lightly beaten

2 tsp baking powder

4 tbsp coconut flour

1 cup broccoli florets, chopped

1 cup cheddar cheese, shredded

Directions:

Preheat the oven to 350 F.

Add all **Ingredients** into the bowl and mix well.

Pour egg mixture into the prepared loaf pan and bake in oven for 30 minutes.

Slice and serve.

Shrimp Green Beans

Preparation Time: 10 minutes

Serve: 4

Ingredients:

1 lb shrimp, peeled and deveined

1 ½ tbsp soy sauce

2 tbsp olive oil

1/2 lb green beans, trimmed

Salt

Directions:

Heat oil in a pan over medium-high heat.

Add beans to the pan and sauté for 5-6 minutes.

Remove pan from heat and set aside.

Add shrimp in the same pan and sauté for 2-3 minutes each side.

Return beans to the pan.

Add soy sauce and stir well and cook shrimp is completely cooked.

Season with salt. Serve.

Leek Mushroom Frittata

Preparation Time: 10 minutes

Serve: 4

Ingredients:

6 eggs

1 cup leeks, sliced

6 oz mushrooms, sliced

Pepper

Salt

Directions:

Preheat the oven to 350 F.

Spray pan with cooking spray and heat over medium heat.

Add mushrooms, leeks, and salt in a pan sauté for 6 minutes.

Whisk eggs in a bowl with pepper and salt.

Transfer sautéed mushroom and leek mixture into the greased baking dish.

Pour egg mixture over mushroom.

Bake in oven for 40 minutes.

Serve and enjoy.

Italian Casserole

Preparation Time: 10 minutes

Serve: 4

Ingredients:

2 eggs

2/3 cup parmesan cheese, grated

2/3 cup chicken broth

1 lb Italian sausage

4 egg whites

4 tsp pine nuts, minced

¼ cup roasted red pepper, sliced

¼ cup pesto sauce

1/8 tsp pepper

¼ tsp sea salt

Directions:

Preheat the oven to 400 F.

Add sausage in pan and cook until golden brown. Drain excess oil and spread it into the greased casserole dish.

Whisk remaining **Ingredients** except pine nuts in a bowl and pour over sausage.

Bake in oven for 35 minutes.

Garnish with pine nuts and serve.

Cauliflower Cheese Grits

Preparation Time: 10 minutes

Serve: 8

Ingredients:

6 cups cauliflower rice

1/2 cup vegetable broth

1 cup cream cheese

1/2 tsp pepper

1 tsp salt

Directions:

Add all Ingredients to the crock pot and stir well combine.

Cover slow cooker with lid and cook on low for 2 hours.

Stir well and serve.

Flax Pumpkin Muffins

Preparation Time: 5 minutes

Serve: 2

Ingredients:

1 egg

2 tbsp swerve

2 tbsp ground flaxseed

2 tbsp almond flour

1 1/2 tsp pumpkin spice

1/4 tsp baking powder

2 tbsp pumpkin puree

Directions:

Grease two ramekins with butter.

In a bowl, mix together pumpkin puree and egg.

In separate bowl, mix together almond flour, pumpkin spice, baking powder, swerve, and ground flaxseed.

Pour pumpkin and egg mixture into the almond flour mixture and mix well.

Pour mixture into the prepared ramekins and microwave for 1-2 minutes.

Serve and enjoy.

Chapter 7: Pork,Lamb and Beef Recipes

Italian Pork Chops

Preparation Time: 10 minutes

Serve: 4

Ingredients:

4 pork loin chops, boneless

2 garlic cloves, minced

1 tsp Italian seasoning

1 tbsp fresh rosemary, chopped

1/4 tsp black pepper

1/2 tsp kosher salt

Directions:

Season pork chops with pepper and salt.

In a small bowl, mix together garlic, Italian seasoning, and rosemary.

Rub Pork chops with garlic and rosemary mixture.

Place pork chops on a baking tray and roast in oven at 425 F for 10 minutes.

Turn temperature to 350 F and roast for 25 minutes more

Serve and enjoy.

Cinnamon Olive Pork Chops

Preparation Time: 10 minutes

Serve: 6

Ingredients:

6 pork chops, boneless and cut into thick slices

1/2 cup olives, pitted and sliced

7.5 oz ragu

1 tbsp olive oil

1/4 cup beef broth

3 garlic cloves, chopped

1/8 tsp ground cinnamon

1 large onion, sliced

Directions:

Heat oil in a pan over medium-high heat.

Add pork chops in a pan and cook until lightly brown and set aside.

Cook garlic and onion and cook until onion is softened.

Add broth and bring to boil.

Return pork chops to pan and stir in ragu and remaining **Ingredients**.

Cover and simmer for 20 minutes.

Serve and enjoy.

Pork Egg Roll Bowl

Preparation Time: 10 minutes

Serve: 6

Ingredients:

1 lb ground pork

3 tbsp soy sauce

1 tbsp sesame oil

1/2 onion, sliced

1 medium cabbage head, sliced

2 tbsp green onion, chopped

2 tbsp chicken broth

1 tsp ground ginger

2 garlic cloves, minced

Pepper

Salt

Directions:

Brown meat in a pan over medium heat.

Add oil and onion to the pan with meat. Mix well and cook over medium heat.

In a small bowl, mix together soy sauce, ginger, and garlic.

Add soy sauce mixture to the pan.

Add cabbage to the pan and toss to coat.

Add broth to the pan and mix well.

Cook over medium heat for 3 minutes.

Season with pepper and salt.

Garnish with green onion and serve.

Herb Pork Chops

Preparation Time: 10 minutes

Cooking Time: 30 minutes

Serve: 4

Ingredients:

4 pork chops, boneless

1 tbsp olive oil

2 garlic cloves, minced

1 tsp dried rosemary, crushed

1 tsp oregano

½ tsp thyme

1 tbsp fresh rosemary, chopped

¼ tsp pepper

¼ tsp salt

Directions:

Preheat the oven 425 F.

Season pork chops with pepper and salt and set aside.

In a small bowl, mix together garlic, oil, rosemary, oregano, thyme, and fresh rosemary and rub over pork chops.

Place pork chops on baking tray and roast for 10 minutes.

Turn heat to 350 F and roast for 25 minutes more.

Serve and enjoy.

Greek Pork Chops

Preparation Time: 10 minutes

Cooking Time: 20 minutes

Serve: 4

Ingredients:

4 pork chops, boneless

1 cup feta cheese, crumbled

2 zucchini, sliced

1 cup chicken stock

2 tsp oregano

1 tbsp garlic, minced

¼ cup olives, cut in half

2 cups cherry tomatoes, halved

¼ cup olive oil

Directions:

Season pork chops with pepper and salt.

Heat 2 tablespoons of oil in a pan over medium heat.

Add pork chops to the pan and cook until lightly brown from both the sides, about 3-5 minutes. Transfer pork chops on a plate.

Add remaining oil to the pan.

Add zucchini and cook 5 minutes.

Add garlic and sauté for 30 seconds.

Add oregano and stock and simmer for 2 minutes.

Set zucchini one side of the pan.

Return pork chops to the pan and cook until chops are no longer pink.

Transfer zucchini and pork chops to a plate.

Add olive and tomatoes to the pan and stir for a minute.

Pour olive and tomatoes over pork chops.

Top with feta cheese and serve.

Chapter 8: Fish Recipes

Shrimp Scampi

Preparation Time: 10 minutes

Cooking Time: 10 minutes

Serve: 4

Ingredients:

1 lb shrimp

1/4 tsp red pepper flakes

1 tbsp fresh lemon juice

1/4 cup butter

1/2 cup chicken broth

2 garlic cloves, minced

1 shallot, sliced

3 tbsp olive oil

3 tbsp parsley, chopped

Pepper

Salt

Directions:

Heat oil in a pan over medium heat.

Add garlic and shallots and cook for 3 minutes.

Add broth, lemon juice, and butter and cook for 5 minutes.

Add red pepper flakes, parsley, pepper, and salt. Stir.

Add shrimp and cook for 3 minutes.

Serve and enjoy.

Shrimp and Broccoli

Preparation Time: 10 minutes

Cooking Time: 7 minutes

Serve: 2

Ingredients:

1/2 lb shrimp

1 tsp fresh lemon juice

2 tbsp butter

2 garlic cloves, minced

1 cup broccoli florets

Salt

Directions:

Melt butter in a pan over medium heat.

Add garlic and broccoli to pan and cook for 3-4 minutes.

Add shrimp and cook for 3-4 minutes.

Add lemon juice and salt and stir well.

Serve and enjoy.

Baked Salmon

Preparation Time: 10 minutes

Cooking Time: 35 minutes

Serve: 4

Ingredients:

1 lb salmon fillet

4 tbsp parsley, chopped

1/4 cup mayonnaise

1/4 cup parmesan cheese, grated

2 garlic cloves, minced

2 tbsp butter

Directions:

Preheat the oven to 350 F.

Place salmon on greased baking tray.

Melt butter in a pan over medium heat.

Add garlic and sauté for minute.

Add remaining ingredient and stir to combined.

Spread pan mixture over salmon fillet.

Bake for 20-25 minutes.

Serve and enjoy.

Nutritional Value (Amount per Serving):

Calories 412

Fat 26 g

Carbohydrates 4.3 g

Sugar 1 g

Protein 34 g

Cholesterol 99 mg

Avocado Shrimp Salad

Preparation Time: 10 minutes

Cooking Time: 10 minutes

Serve: 6

Ingredients:

1 lb shrimp

3 bacon slices, cooked and crumbled

1/4 cup feta cheese, crumbled

1 tbsp lemon juice

1/2 cup tomatoes, chopped

2 avocados, chopped

2 garlic cloves, minced

1 tbsp olive oil

Pepper

Salt

Directions:

Heat oil in a pan over medium heat.

Add garlic and sauté for minute.

Add shrimp, pepper, and salt and cook for 5-7 minutes. Remove from heat and set aside.

Meanwhile, add remaining **Ingredients** to the large mixing bowl.

Add shrimp and toss well.

Cover and place in fridge for 1 hour.

Serve and enjoy.

Nutritional Value (Amount per Serving):

Calories 268

Fat 18 g

Carbohydrates 8.1 g

Sugar 1.1 g

Protein 19.6 g

Cholesterol 165 mg

Chapter 9: Keto Recipes for Vegetable Recipes

Broccoli and Tomatoes

Preparation Time: 22 minutes,

servings: 6

Ingredients:

1 tsp Chili flakes .

1 Broccoli head with florets separated

4 Cubed tomatoes

1 cup Veggie stock

1 cup Cauliflower rice

2 tsp Curry powder .

1 tbsp Grated ginger .

Directions:

Mix all the **Ingredients** in the instant pot and seal the lid to cook at high pressure for 12 minutes.

Natural release the pressure for 10 minutes, share into bowls and serve.

Cabbage Sautè

Preparation Time: 20 minutes

Serves: 2-4

Ingredients

Cabbage:

1/3 small head white cabbage, cored and shredded

2 tbsp olive oil

Salt to taste

Sauce:

¼ cup peanut butter, at room temperature

1/3 tsp minced garlic

1/3 tbsp lime juice

1 tbsp water

1/3 tsp ginger, minced

1/3 tsp cayenne pepper

1 tbsp rice wine vinegar

1/3 tbsp chilli sauce

Directions

Heat 2 tbsp of olive oil in a saucepan over medium heat and add the cabbage, 2 tbsp of water and pinch of salt. Cook until wilted and remove to a plate. Whisk the peanut butter with the remaining sauce **Ingredients** in a bowl. Set aside.

Sesame Savoy Cabbage

Preparation Time: 20 minutes

Servings: 3

Ingredients

2 medium Savoy Cabbages, finely chopped

1 tablespoon sesame oil

2 small Onions, chopped

2 cups Bacon, chopped

2 ½ cups Mixed Bone Broth, see recipe above

¼ tsp Mace

2 cups Coconut Milk

1 Bay Leaf

Salt to taste

3 tbsp Chopped Parsley

Directions

Set on Sauté. Add the bacon crumbles, sesame oil and onions; cook until crispy. Add bone broth and scrape the bottom of the pot. Stir in bay leaf and cabbage. Cut out some parchment paper and cover the cabbage with it.

Seal the lid, select Manual mode and cook on High Pressure for 4 minutes. Once ready, press Cancel and quickly release the pressure. Select Sauteé, stir in the milk and nutmeg. Simmer for 5 minutes, add the parsley.

Cabbage Soup

Preparation time: 20 minutes

Servings: 4

Ingredients:

1-pound green cabbage, shredded

1 shallot, chopped

12 cups chicken stock

1 celery stalk, chopped

1 tablespoon olive oil

A pinch of salt and black pepper

2 tablespoons dill, chopped

Directions:

Set your instant pot on sauté mode, add oil, heat it up, add the shallot and sauté for 2 minutes.

Add the rest of the **Ingredients**, put the lid on and cook on High for 13 minutes. Release the pressure fast for 6 minutes, ladle the soup into bowls and serve.

Zucchini Cream

Preparation Time: 22 minutes,

Servings: 4

Ingredients:

4 Sliced zucchini

1 tbsp Chopped dill .

½ cup Veggie stock

½ cup Softened cream cheese

½ cup Heavy cream

A pinch of salt and black pepper

1 tbsp Avocado oil .

2 cloves Minced garlic

Directions:

Put the zucchini in the instant pot and mix in the stock, salt, and pepper then seal the lid to cook for 12 minutes at high pressure.

Natural release the pressure for 10 minutes, strain the zucchini and put it in a food processor. Mix in the rest of the

Ingredients and blend well. Share into bowls and serve as a spread.

Marinated Kale Salad

Preparation Time: 5 minutes

Servings: 4

Ingredients:

For salad:

- 2 bunches curly kale

- 5 tablespoons apple cider vinegar

- 2 tablespoons agave nectar or pure maple syrup

- 2 tablespoons natural almond butter

- 2 – 4 tablespoons tamari or soy sauce or coconut aminos

Optional toppings:

- ½ cup cherry tomatoes

- 2 tablespoons pepitas

- 1 avocado, peeled, pitted, chopped

- Any other toppings of your choice

Directions:

- Dry the kale leaves by patting with a kitchen towel.

- Tear the kale into bite size pieces and place in a large bowl.

- Add rest of the Ingredients for salad into a bowl and whisk well.

- Drizzle the dressing over the kale leaves and mix it well using your hands, massaging the leaves lightly.

- Divide into 4 meal prep containers and refrigerate until use. It can last for a day.

Pea Soup

Preparation Time: 10 minutes

Servings: 4

Ingredients:

- 2 onions, chopped

- 2 large potatoes, peeled, cubed

- 6 cups vegetable broth or water

- 2 large cloves garlic, peeled, sliced

- 1.3 pounds peas, fresh or frozen

- 2 tablespoons vegetable oil

- A handful fresh parsley or any other herbs of your choice, chopped

- Salt to taste

- Pepper to taste

Serving day **Ingredients**:

- ½ cup boiled peas

- Vegan yogurt or vegan cream, to drizzle

- Any other toppings of your choice

- 2 tablespoons lemon juice

Directions:

Place a soup pot over medium heat. Add oil. When the oil is heated, add onion and garlic and sauté until pink.

Stir in the stock, salt, pepper, parsley, potatoes and peas. When it begins to boil, lower the heat and cover with a lid. Cook until potatoes are soft. Turn off the heat.

Blend with an immersion blender until smooth. Let it cool completely.

Transfer into an airtight container and refrigerate until use. It can last for 4 days. You can also pour into freezer bags. Label and seal the bags and freeze until use. It can last for 2 months.

To serve: Heat thoroughly. Add lemon juice and stir. Ladle into soup bowls. Garnish with peas, vegan yogurt and any other toppings of your choice and serve.

Chapter 10: Appetizer and Snack Recipes

Keto Tacos

Preparation Time: 24 Minutes

Servings: 6

Ingredients:

One pound of beef (lean ground)

3 tablespoon of taco seasoning mix

Two tablespoons of cilantro

One small can green chilies (diced)

One can of Rotel

One packet of frozen veggies

Directions:

Take out your instant pot and add beef in it. Stir until well combined

Now put all the other Ingredients in the beef, except for cheese. Mix well.

Close your instant pot and cook the taco dip for 2 minutes on high-pressure mode. When the cooking is done quickly release the steam.

Open the instant pot and mix the cheese in it. Stir until well combined.

Your taco dip is ready. Enjoy

Nutritional Data Per Serving:

Fat: 7 gram

Fiber: 2 gram

Carbohydrates: 9 gram

Sugar: 1 gram

Protein: 17 gram.

Avocado Salsa

Preparation Time: 1 hour and 10 minutes

Servings: 6

Ingredients:

2 lbs. beef chuck roast, cut into strips

1 tablespoon taco seasoning

2 tablespoons coconut oil

2 cans diced green chilies with juice

Cabbage Slaw & Dressing **Ingredients**:

½ a small head of cabbage

1 small green cabbage

½ cup thinly sliced green onion

2 teaspoons green tabasco sauce

6 tablespoons mayo

4 teaspoons lime juice, fresh squeezed

Avocado Salsa **Ingredients**:

2 large avocados, diced

1 tablespoon lime juice, fresh squeezed

1 medium Poblano pepper, diced very small

1 tablespoon extra-virgin olive oil

1 cup cilantro, freshly chopped

Directions:

Remove all excess fat from the meat and cut into strips. Season the meat strips with taco seasoning. Set your instant pot to sauté mode. Add in coconut oil and meat, sauté until meat is no longer pink and browned on all sides.

Press the keep warm/cancel button to stop sauté once the meat is browned. Set to meat/stew setting for 1 hour. Release the pressure naturally. Remove the meat from instant pot and shred on chopping board with a fork.

Place shredded meat back into your instant pot and replace the lid and keep on the keep warm/cancel setting. Slice the cabbage and the green onions to tiny strips using a slicer.

Make the dressing by whisking the green Tabasco, mayo, and lime juice together. Mix the strips of cabbage and onions with the dressing. Slice the avocados and mix with lime juice.

Chop cilantro and Poblano pepper very finely, and mix with the avocado. Pour in olive oil and mix. Place slaw in serving bowls. Top with beef and avocado salsa. Serve.

Walnut Fat Bombs

Servings: 10

Preparation Time: 10 minutes

Ingredients

2 tablespoons keto chocolate protein powder

1/4 cup Erythritol

5 ounces butter

3 ounces walnut butter

10 whole walnuts, halved

Directions

In a sauté pan, melt the butter, protein powder, and Erythritol over a low flame; stir until smooth and well mixed.

Spoon the mixture into a piping bag and pipe into mini cupcake liners. Add the walnut halves to each mini cupcake.

Place in your refrigerator for at least 2 hours. Bon appétit!

Bacon Avocado Sushi

Servings: 8

Preparation Time: 15 minutes

Ingredients

1 teaspoon garlic paste

2 scallions, finely chopped

4 ounces cream cheese, softened

1 teaspoon adobo sauce

1 avocado, mashed

2 tablespoons fresh lemon juice

8 bacon slices

1 tablespoon toasted sesame seeds

Directions

In a mixing bowl, thoroughly combine the garlic paste, scallions, cream cheese, adobo sauce, avocado, and fresh lemon juice.

Divide the mixture evenly between the bacon slices. Roll up tightly and garnish with toasted sesame seeds. Enjoy!

Ham and Avocado Stuffed Eggs

Preparation Time: 20 minutes

Servings: 4

Ingredients

4 large eggs

1/2 avocado, mashed

1/2 teaspoon yellow mustard

1 garlic clove, minced

2 ounces cooked ham, chopped

Directions

Place the eggs in a saucepan and fill with enough water. Bring the water to a rolling boil; heat off. Cover and allow the eggs to sit for about 12 minutes; let them cool.

Slice the eggs into halves; mix the yolks with the avocado, mustard and garlic.

Dive the avocado filling among the egg whites. Top with the chopped ham. Bon appétit!

Saucy and Spicy Spareribs

Preparation Time: 20 minutes

Servings: 4

Ingredients

2 pounds St. Louis-style spareribs

1 tablespoon Fajita seasoning mix

2 cloves garlic, pressed

1/2 cup chicken bone broth

1 cup tomato sauce

Directions

Toss the spareribs with the Fajita seasoning mix, garlic, chicken bone broth, and tomato sauce until well coated.

Arrange the spare ribs on a tinfoil-lined baking sheet.

Bake in the preheated oven at 260 degrees F for 2 hours and 30 minutes.

Place under the preheated broiler for about 8 minutes until the sauce is lightly caramelized. Bon appétit!

Two Cheese and Prosciutto Balls

Preparation Time: 10 minutes

Servings: 4

Ingredients

2 ounces goat cheese, crumbled

2 ounces feta cheese crumbled

3 ounces prosciutto, chopped

1 red bell pepper, deveined and finely chopped

2 tablespoons sesame seeds, toasted

Directions

Thoroughly combine the cheese, prosciutto and pepper until everything is well incorporated. Shape the mixture into balls.

Arrange these keto balls on a platter and place them in the refrigerator until ready to serve.

Roll the keto balls in toasted sesame seeds before serving. Bon appétit!

Stuffed Mini Peppers

Preparation Time: 20 minutes

Servings: 6

Ingredients

3/4 pound ground beef

1/2 cup onion, chopped

2 garlic cloves, minced

12 mini peppers, deveined

1/2 cup cheddar cheese, shredded

Directions

Heat up a lightly oiled sauté pan over a moderate flame. Brown the ground beef for 3 to 4 minutes, crumbling with a fork.

Stir in the onions and garlic; continue to sauté an additional 2 minutes or until tender and aromatic.

Cook the peppers in boiling water until just tender or approximately 7 minutes.

Arrange the stuffed peppers on a tinfoil-lined baking pan. Divide the beef mixture among the peppers. Top with the shredded cheddar cheese.

Bake in the preheated oven at 360 degrees F approximately 17 minutes. Serve at room temperature. Bon appétit!

Homemade Wings in Spicy Tomato Sauce

Servings: 6

Preparation Time: 50 minutes

Ingredients

3 pounds chicken wings

Sea salt and ground black pepper, to taste

1/2 teaspoon paprika

1/2 teaspoon cayenne pepper

Sauce:

2 vine-ripe tomatoes

1 onion

2 garlic cloves

1 teaspoon chili pepper

Directions

Start by preheating your oven to 400 degrees F. Set a wire rack inside a rimmed baking sheet.

Season the chicken wings with salt, black pepper, paprika, and cayenne pepper. Bake the wings approximately 45 minutes or until the skin is crispy.

To make the sauce, puree all **Ingredients** in your food processor. Bon appétit!

Chapter 11: Keto Desserts

Peanut Butter

Preparation Time: 15 minutes

Servings: 1

Ingredients

¼ tsp. salt

4 tbsp. erythritol

½ cup peanut butter

1 egg

Directions:

Combine the salt, erythritol, and peanut butter in a bowl, incorporating everything well. Break the egg over the mixture and mix to create a dough.

Flatten the dough using a rolling pin and cut into shapes with a knife or cookie cutter. Make a crisscross on the top of each cookie with a fork.

Pre-heat your fryer at 360°F.

Once the fryer has warmed up, put the cookies inside and leave to cook for ten minutes. Take care when taking them out and allow to cook before enjoying.

Lemon Custard

Preparation Time: 10 minutes

Serve: 4

Ingredients:

2 ½ cups heavy cream

2 tbsp fresh lime juice

¼ cup fresh lemon juice

½ cup Swerve

½ tsp orange extract

Pinch of salt

Directions:

Boil heavy cream and sweetener in a saucepan for 5-6 minutes. Stir constantly.

Turn off the heat and add orange extract, lime juice, lemon juice, and salt and mix well.

Pour custard mixture into ramekins and place in refrigerator for 6 hours.

Serve chilled and enjoy.

Keto Chocolate Mousse

Preparation Time: 5 minutes

Servings: 2

Ingredients:

1 cup heavy whipping cream

¼ cup unsweetened cocoa powder, sifted

¼ cup Swerve powdered sweetener

1 tsp vanilla extract

¼ tsp kosher salt

Directions:

Add cream to the bowl of an electric stand mixture and beat it until it forms peaks.

Stir in cocoa powder, vanilla, sweetener, and salt.

Mix well until smooth.

Refrigerate for 4 hours.

Serve.

Peanut Butter Chocolate Bars

Preparation Time: 10 minutes

Serve: 24

Ingredients

5 eggs

1 cup walnuts, chopped

¼ cup coconut flour

2 tsp vanilla

½ cup peanut butter

8.5 oz cream cheese

2 cups erythritol

1 cup unsweetened chocolate chips

1 ½ tsp baking powder

1 cup almond flour

Pinch of salt

Directions:

Preheat the oven to 350 F.

In a bowl, beat together peanut butter, sweetener, vanilla, and cream cheese until smooth.

Add eggs and beat until well combined.

Add remaining **Ingredients** and stir gently to combine.

Transfer mixture to the greased cookie sheet and spread evenly.

Bake in oven for 35 minutes.

Allow to cool completely.

Slice and serve.

Chia Almond Pudding

Preparation Time: 5 minutes

Serve: 4

Ingredients:

2 tbsp almonds, toasted and crushed

1/3 cup chia seeds

½ tsp vanilla

4 tbsp erythritol

¼ cup unsweetened cocoa powder

2 cups unsweetened almond milk

Directions:

Add almond milk, vanilla, sweetener, and cocoa powder into the blender and blend until well combined.

Pour blended mixture into the bowl.

Add chia seeds and whisk for 1-2 minutes.

Pour pudding mixture into the serving bowls and place in fridge for 1-2 hours.

Top with crushed almonds and serve.

Blackberry Ice Cream

Preparation Time: 5 minutes

Serve: 8

Ingredients:

1 cup blackberries

1 egg yolks

½ cup erythritol

1 ½ cup heavy whipping cream

Directions:

Add all **Ingredients** to the bowl and blend until well combined.

Pour ice cream mixture into the ice cream maker and churn ice cream according to the machine instructions.

Serve chilled and enjoy.

Chocolate Fat Bombs

Preparation Time: 5 minutes

Serve: 8

Ingredients:

125g/4.4 ounces of cream cheese

125g/4.4 ounces of unsalted butter

2 tablespoons cacao powder

1 tablespoon of sweetener

Directions:

Spot the cream cheddar and margarine into an enormous bowl and leave it to cool delicately at room temperature.

At the point when softened, beat quickly with an electric whisk at that point and add the cacao powder and your sugar according to taste.

Beat until smooth.

Get out mini baking cups and spot 1-2 teaspoons of the blend into each cup.

Place it into the refrigerator to solidify and enjoy!

Quick Matcha Latte

Preparation Time: 5 minutes

Serve: 2

Ingredients:

½ tsp Latte

2 tbsp swerve

1 tsp matcha powder

1 cup heavy whipping cream

Directions:

Add all Ingredients into the glass jar.

Seal jar with lid and shake for 4-5 minutes until mixture double.

Place in refrigerator for 3-4 hours.

Serve chilled and enjoy.

Conclusion

To close out this guide, I want to leave you with a few short words of advice and motivation. The first time you start this diet it might feel easy because of motivation. Motivation tends to die down after the first couple of days and than you are left to exercise discipline. It may start to feel sacrificial when your friends or family are eating pizza and your stuck eating a salad.

You are going to second guess your new choice over and over and wonder if you're doing the right thing. This is all completely normal. The next thing is that Keto is not for everyone, but it is likely that it is for you if you've made it this far!

Don't try to convince your husband and kids to join you if they aren't ready and don't pressure your best friends either. Do this for you. The best way to change others is to change yourself and let your success be contagious and desirable for others to see. Lastly, don't become unsocial because your afraid of food and being around others.

CPSIA information can be obtained
at www.ICGtesting.com
Printed in the USA
BVHW062221190321
603092BV00004B/366